2015

TPA Department/Insurance Help Desk In A Hospital

Adnan Mastan

BUMS, MD (Medicine),

FIII, DHI, DHM, DLU

TPA Department/Insurance Help Desk In A Hospital

Name of the Book: TPA Department/Insurance Help Desk In A Hospital

Name of the Author: Dr.Adnan Mastan

Published: August 2015

Edition: First

Note: As new information becomes available, changes become necessary. The editors/author/contributors have, as far as it is possible, taken care to ensure that the information given in this book is accurate and up-to-date. In view of the possibility of human error or advances in medical science neither the author nor the publisher nor any other party who has been involved in the preparation or publication of this work warrants that the information contained herein is in every respect accurate or complete. Readers are strongly advised to confirm.

Printed in USA

Preface

Third party administrators are the new breed of intermediaries in the insurance sector, TPA deptt. in a hospital is established to facilitate the health insurance needs of the patients. This book is aimed to provide concise introduction of the TPA department/Insurance help desk in a hospital along with specific mention to basic approaches for better management of the department. It is hoped that this book shall provide evidence based guidelines about procedure and structure of TPA department/Insurance help desk in a hospital to all readers.

I am highly indebted to my friends and colleagues for providing the necessary stimulus for writing this book. I am grateful to all those persons whose writings and works have helped me in the preparation of this book. I am equally grateful to the reviewer of the manuscript of this book who made extremely valuable suggestions and has thus contributed in enhancing the standard of the book. I shall feel amply rewarded if the book proves helpful to the readers. I look forward to suggestions from all readers for further improving the subject content as well as the presentation of this book.

Adnan Mastan

Contents

INTRODUCTION

The term health insurance is generally used to describe a form of insurance that pays for medical expenses. It is sometimes used more broadly to include insurance covering disability or long-term nursing or custodial care needs. It may be provided through a government-sponsored social insurance program, or from private insurance companies. It may be purchased on a group basis (e.g., by a firm to cover its employees) or purchased by individual consumers. In each case, the covered groups or individuals pay premiums or taxes to help protect themselves from high or unexpected healthcare expenses. Similar benefits paying for medical expenses may also be provided through social welfare programs funded by the government.

In light of the fiscal crisis facing the government at both central and state levels, in the form of shrinking public health budgets, escalating health care costs coupled with demand for health-care services, and lack of easy access of people from the low-income group to quality health care, health insurance is emerging as an alternative mechanism for financing of health care and now it's very much evident that most of the hospital business depends on Health insurance patients so it is more so important to provide a better processing of health insurance request of patients as it's the revenue generating department of hospital and today, most Health Insurance policies do offer cashless hospitalization facility and route your policy through a Third party Administrator (TPA). However you should be familiar with the terms- Network Hospital and Non-network Hospital.

HEALTH INSURANCE IN INDIA: CURRENT SCENARIO

The health care system in India is characterized by multiple systems of Medicine, mixed ownership patterns and different kinds of delivery structures. Public sector ownership is divided between central and state governments, Municipal and *Panchayat* local governments. Public health facilities include Teaching hospitals, secondary level hospitals, first-level referral hospitals (CHCs or rural hospitals), dispensaries; primary health centers (PHCs), sub-centers, and health posts. Also included are public facilities for selected occupational Groups like organized work force (ESI), defence, government employees (CGHS), railways, post and telegraph and mines among others. The private sector (for profit and not for profit) is the dominant sector with 50 per cent of people seeking indoor care and around 60 to 70 per cent of those seeking ambulatory care (or outpatient care) from private health facilities. While India has made significant gains in terms of health indicators - demographic, infrastructural and epidemiological (See Tables 1 and 2), This is coupled with spiraling health costs, high financial burden on the poor and erosion in their incomes. Around 24% of all people hospitalized in India in a single year fall below the poverty line due to hospitalization *(World Bank, 2002).* India spends about 4.9% of GDP on *(Regional Overview in South-East Asia)* health *(WHR, 2002).* The per capita total expenditure on health in India is US$ 23, of which the per capita Government expenditure on health is US$ 4.Hence, it is seen that the total health expenditure is around 5% of GDP, with breakdown of public expenditure (0.9%); private expenditure (4.0%). The private expenditure can be further classified as out-of-pocket (OOP) expenditure (3.6%) and employees/community financing (0.4%). It is thus evident that public health investment has been comparatively low. In fact as a percentage of GDP it has declined from 1.3% in 1990 to 0.9% as at present. Furthermore, the central budgetary allocation for health (as a percentage of the total Central budget) has been stagnant at 1.3% while in the states it has declined from 7.0% to 5.5%.

Table 1. Socioeconomic indicators

Land area	2% of world area
Burden of disease (%)	21% of global disease burden
Population	16% of world population
Urban : Rural	28:72
Literacy rate (%)	65.38
Sanitation (%)	Rural – 9.0; Urban – 49.3
Safe drinking water supply (%)	Rural – 98; Urban – 90.2
Poverty (%)	Below poverty line – 26
	Rural – 27.09; Urban – 23.62
Poverty line (Rs.)	Rural – 327.56; Urban – 454.11

Table 2. Achievements: 1951-2000

Demographic changes	1951	1981	2000
Life expectancy	36.7	54	64.6 (RGI)
Crude birth rate	40.8	33.9 (SRS)	26.1 (99 SRS)
Crude death rate	25	12.5 (SRS)	8.7 (99 SRS)
Infant mortality rate	146	110	70 (99 SRS)

Epidemiology	1951	1981	2000
Malaria (cases in millions)	75	2.7	2.2
Leprosy cases per 10,000 Population	38.1	57.3	3.74
Small pox (no of cases)	>44,887	Eradicated	Eradicated
Guinea worm (no. of cases)	>39,792	Eradicated	Eradicated
Polio		29709	265

Infrastructure	1951	1981	2000
SC/PHC/CHC	725	57,363	1,63,181(99-RHS)
Dispensaries & hospitals(all)	9209	23,555	43,322 (95–96-CBHI)
Beds (Pvt & Public)	117,198	569,495	8,70,161 (95-96-CBHI)
Doctors (Allopathic)	61,800	2,68,700	5,03,900 (98-99-MCI)
Nursing personnel	18,054	1,43,887	7,37,000 (99-INC)

HEALTH INSURANCE

Health insurance in a narrow sense would be 'an individual or group purchasing health care coverage in advance by paying a fee called *premium.*' In its broader sense, it would be any arrangement that helps to defer, delay, reduce or altogether avoid payment for health care incurred by individuals and households. The health insurance market in India is very limited covering about 10% of the total population. The existing schemes can be categorized as:

1. Voluntary health insurance schemes or private-for-profit schemes;

2. Employer-based schemes;

3. Insurance offered by NGOs / community based health insurance, and

4. Mandatory health insurance schemes or government run schemes (namely ESIS, CGHS).

Voluntary health insurance schemes or private-for-profit schemes

In private insurance, buyers are willing to pay premium to an insurance company that pools people with similar risks and insures them for health expenses. The key distinction is that the premiums are set at a level, which provides a profit to third party and provider institutions. Premiums are based on an assessment of the risk status of the consumer (or of the group of employees) and the level of benefits provided, rather than as a proportion of the consumer's income.

In the public sector, the General Insurance Corporation (GIC) and its four subsidiary companies (National Insurance Corporation, New India Assurance Company, Oriental Insurance Company and United Insurance Company) and the Life Insurance Corporation (LIC) of India provide voluntary insurance schemes.

Of the various schemes offered, Mediclaim is the main product of the GIC. The Medical Insurance Scheme or Med claim was introduced in November 1986 and it covers individuals and groups with persons aged 5 – 80 yrs. Children (3 months – 5 yrs) are covered with their parents. This scheme provides for reimbursement of medical expenses (now offers cashless scheme) by an individual towards hospitalization and domiciliary hospitalization as per the sum insured. There are exclusions and pre-existing disease clauses. Premiums are calculated based on age and the sum insured, which in turn varies from Rs 15 000 to Rs 5 00 000. In 1995/96 about half a million Mediclaim policies were issued with about 1.8 million beneficiaries (Krause Patrick 2000). The coverage for the year 2000-01 was around 7.2 million.

The year 1999 marked the beginning of a new era for health insurance in the Indian context. With the passing of the Insurance Regulatory Development Authority Bill (IRDA) the insurance sector was opened to private and foreign participation, thereby paving the way for the entry of private health insurance companies. The Bill also facilitated the establishment of an authority to protect the interests of the insurance holders by regulating, promoting and ensuring orderly growth of the insurance industry. The bill allows foreign promoters to hold paid up capital of up to 26 percent in an Indian company and requires them to have a capital of Rs 100 crore along with a business plan to begin its operations. Currently, a few companies such as Bajaj Alliance, ICICI, Royal Sundaram, and Cholamandalam among others are offering health insurance schemes. Karnataka 7 000 Health Insurance

HEALTH INSURANCE SCENARIO IN OTHER COUNTRIES

Health insurance in Australia

The public health system is called Medicare. It ensures free universal access to hospital treatment and subsidized out-of-hospital medical treatment. It is funded by a 1.5% tax levy.

The private health system is funded by a number of private health insurance organizations. The largest of these is Medibank Private, which is government-owned, but operates as a government business enterprise under the same regulatory regime as all other registered private health funds. The Coalition Howard government had announced that Medibank would be privatized if it won the 2007 election, however they were defeated by the Australian Labor Party under Kevin Rudd which had already pledged that it would remain in government ownership.

Some private health insurers are 'for profit' enterprises, and some are non-profit organizations such as HCF Health Insurance. Some have membership restricted to particular groups, but the majority has open membership.

Most aspects of private health insurance in Australia are regulated by the *Private Health Insurance Act 2007*.

The private health system in Australia operates on a "community rating" basis, whereby premiums do not vary solely because of a person's previous medical history, current state of health or (generally speaking) their age (but see Lifetime Health Cover below). Balancing this are waiting periods, in particular for pre-existing conditions (usually referred to within the industry as PEA, which stands for "pre-existing ailment"). Funds are entitled to impose a waiting period of up to 12 months on benefits for any medical condition the signs and symptoms of which existed during the six months ending on the day the person first took out insurance. They are also entitled to impose a 12-month waiting period for benefits for treatment relating to an obstetric condition, and a 2-month waiting period for all other benefits when a person first takes out private insurance. Funds have the discretion to reduce or remove such waiting periods in individual cases. They are also free not to impose them to begin with, but this would place such a fund at risk of "adverse selection", attracting a disproportionate number of members from other funds, or from the pool of intending members who might otherwise have joined other funds. It would also attract people with existing medical conditions, who might not otherwise have taken out insurance at all because of the denial of benefits for 12 months due to the PEA Rule. The benefits paid out for these conditions would create pressure on premiums for all the fund's members, causing some to drop their membership, which would lead to further rises, and a vicious cycle would ensue.

There are a number of other matters about which funds are not permitted to discriminate between members in terms of premiums, benefits or membership - these include racial origin, religion, sex, sexual orientation, nature of employment, and leisure activities. Premiums for a fund's product that is sold in more than one state can vary from state to state, but not within the same state.

The Australian government has introduced a number of incentives to encourage adults to take out private hospital insurance. These include:

- **Lifetime Health Cover**: If a person has not taken out private hospital cover by the 1st July after their 30th birthday, then when (and if) they do so after this time, their premiums must include a loading of 2% per annum. Thus, a person taking out private cover for the first time at age 40 will pay a 20 per cent loading. The loading continues for

10 years. The loading applies only to premiums for hospital cover, not to ancillary (extras) cover.

- **Medicare Levy Surcharge**: People whose taxable income is greater than a specified amount (currently $50,000 for singles and $100,000 for families) and who do not have an adequate level of private hospital cover must pay a 1% surcharge on top of the standard 1.5% Medicare Levy. The rationale is that if the people in this income group are forced to pay more money one way or another, most would choose to purchase hospital insurance with it, with the possibility of a benefit in the event that they need private hospital treatment - rather than pay it in the form of extra tax as well as having to meet their own private hospital costs.

- **Private Health Insurance Rebate**: The government subsidizes the premiums for all private health insurance cover, including hospital and ancillary (extras), by 30%, 35% or 40%.

Health insurance in Canada

Most health insurance in Canada is administered by each province, under the Canada Health Act, which requires all people to have free access to basic health services. Collectively, the public provincial health insurance systems in Canada are frequently referred to as Medicare. Private health insurance is allowed, but the provincial governments allow it only for services that the public health plans do not cover; for example, semi-private or private rooms in hospitals and prescription drug plans. Canadians are free to use private insurance for elective medical services such as laser vision correction surgery, cosmetic surgery, and other non-basic medical procedures. Some 65% of Canadians have some form of supplementary private health insurance;

many of them receive it through their employers. Private-sector services not paid for by the government account for nearly 30 percent of total health care spending. In 2005, the Supreme Court of Quebec ruled, in Chaoulli v. Quebec, that the province's prohibition on private insurance for health care already insured by the provincial plan could constitute an infringement of the right to life and security if there were long wait times for treatment as happened in this case. Certain other provinces have legislation which financially discourages but does not forbid private health insurance in areas covered by the public plans. The ruling has not changed the overall pattern of health insurance across Canada but has spurred on attempts to tackle the core issues of supply and demand and the impact of wait times.

Health insurance in the Netherlands

In the Netherlands in 2006, a new system of health insurance came into force. All insurance companies have to provide at least one policy which meets a government set minimum standard level of cover and all adult residents are obliged by law to purchase this cover from an insurance company of their choice.

The new system avoids the two pitfalls of adverse selection and moral hazard associated with traditional forms of health insurance.

In the Dutch system, insurance companies are compensated for taking on high risk individuals because they receive extra funding for them. This funding comes from an insurance equalization pool run by a regulator which collects salary based contributions from employers (about 45% of all health care funding) and funding from the government for people whose means are such that they cannot afford health care (about 5% of all funding). Thus insurance companies find that insuring high risk individuals becomes an attractive proposition. All insurance companies receive from the pool, but those with more high risk individuals will receive more from the fund. The remaining 45% of health care funding comes from insurance premiums paid by the public. Insurance companies compete for this money on price alone. The insurance companies are not allowed to set down any co-payments or caps or deductibles. They are not allowed to deny coverage to any person applying for a policy or charge anything other than their nationally set and internet published standard policy premiums. Every person buying insurance from that company will pay the same price as everyone else buying that policy. And every person will get the minimum level of coverage. Children under 18 are insured for free (the funding coming from the equalization pool).

In addition to this minimum level, companies are free to sell extra insurance for additional coverage over the national minimum, but extra risks for this are not covered from the insurance pool and must therefore be priced accordingly.

Health insurance in the United Kingdom

Great Britain's National Health Service (NHS) is a publicly funded healthcare system that provides coverage to everyone normally resident in the UK. The NHS provides the majority of health care in England, including primary care, in-patient care, long-term health care, ophthalmology and dentistry. Private health care has continued parallel to the NHS, paid for largely by private insurance, but it is used by less than 8% of the population, and generally as a top-up to NHS services. Recently the private sector has been increasingly used to increase NHS capacity despite a large proportion of the British public opposing such involvement. According to the World Health Organization, government funding covered 86% of overall health care expenditures in the UK as of 2004, with private expenditures covering the remaining 14%. The costs of running the NHS (est. £104 billion in 2007-8) are met directly from general taxation.

The National Health Service Act 1946 came into effect on 5 July 1948. The UK government department responsible for the NHS is the Department of Health, headed by a Secretary of State for Health (Health Secretary), who sits in the British Cabinet. The NHS is the world's largest health service and the world's third largest employer after the Chinese army and the Indian railways.

Health insurance in the United States

The US market-based health care system relies heavily on private and not-for-profit health insurance, which is the primary source of coverage for most Americans. According to the United States Census Bureau, approximately 84% of Americans have health insurance; some 60% obtain it through an employer, while about 9% purchase it directly. Various government agencies provide coverage to about 27% of Americans (there is some overlap in these figures).

Public programs provide the primary source of coverage for most seniors and for low-income children and families who meet certain eligibility requirements. The primary public programs are Medicare, a federal social insurance program for seniors and certain disabled individuals, Medicaid, funded jointly by the federal government and states but administered at the state level, which covers certain very low income children and their families, and SCHIP, also a federal-state partnership that serves certain children and families who do not qualify for Medicaid but who cannot afford private coverage. Other public programs include military health benefits provided through TRICARE and the Veterans Health Administration and benefits provided through the Indian Health Service. Some states have additional programs for low-income individuals.

In 2006, there were 47 million people in the United States (16% of the population) who were without health insurance for at least part of that year. About 37% of the uninsured live in households with an income over $50,000.

In 2004, US health insurers directly employed almost 470,000 people at an average salary of $61,409. (As of the fourth quarter of 2007, the total US labor force stood at 153.6 million, of whom 146.3 million were employed. Employment related to all forms of insurance totaled 2.3 million. Mean annual earnings for full-time civilian workers in June of 2006 were $41,231; median earnings were $33,634)

CASHLESS HOSPITALIZATION FACILITY

Today, most Health Insurance policies do offer cashless hospitalization facility and route your policy through a Third party Administrator (TPA). However you should be familiar with the terms- Network Hospital and Non-network Hospital. Network Hospitals are those hospitals that your TPA has an agreement with. In case of hospitalization, if you get admitted to a Network Hospital you will be eligible for cashless hospitalization, subject to the other terms and conditions mentioned in your policy being fulfilled. In case you are admitted to a Non-network Hospital, you will have to settle the bills directly to the hospital and then seek re-imbursement through your TPA.

Cashless hospitalization does it mean treatment free of cost?

First, you need to be clear that there is no free treatment. It is just that, in the case of a cashless hospitalization, the insurance company will bear the cost of treatment either fully or partially on your behalf.

Cashless hospitalization is a facility provided by most health insurance policies and enables an insured customer to obtain admission and undergo the required treatment without a direct payment. The assigned TPA will mediate between the healthcare service provider (hospital) and the insurance company and settle the bills on behalf of the insured customer.

However it is important to understand the role of a hospital in cashless hospitalization. The hospital is only a facilitator and has no authority to approve or disapprove any request for cashless hospitalization. Certain protocols laid down by the Insurance Regulatory and Development Authority (IRDA) with respect to cashless hospitalization will need to be adhered to strictly.

Availing the facility of cashless hospitalization

Hospitalization occurs under two circumstances – Planned and Emergency. Pre-authorization of the estimated hospital expense is a must to avail this facility.

Planned Hospitalization:

In the case of a planned admission, you would have first consulted a doctor who in turn would have advised you on the probable date of hospitalization. In such a case, you must have applied for an approval of the estimated hospital expenses directly with your TPA at least 4-5 days prior to the date of hospitalization.

In case you have not applied for a pre-authorization sufficiently in advance or if the doctor treating you advises you to get hospitalized immediately after the consultation, Corporate Help Desk will assist you through the pre-authorization procedure. However, you will need to bear in mind that the Corporate Help Desk/ TPA Deptt. is only a facilitator and can in no way influence the decision on the approval. The approval can be turned down.

The pre-authorization procedure is detailed below:

Step 1: Establish contact with the Corporate TPA Deptt. /Help Desk at the Hospital

Step 2: At the Corporate Help Desk, you need to present the original health Insurance card issued to you by your TPA

Step 3: Collect the pre-authorization will forms pertaining to your TPA

Step 4: Your pre-authorization will have two sections-

i. General details on the health Insurance policy – to be filled in by you (the Corporate desk will assist you in case you have any difficulty)

ii. Pertains to the treatment recommended for you-needs to be filled in and duly signed by the Doctor who is treating you (do not attempt to fill this section, contact the Corporate desk in case of any difficulty)

Step 5: Return the completed form to the Corporate Help Desk. The personnel at the desk will verify the form for its completeness and let you know in case of any discrepancy

Step 6: Once the form is complete in all respects, the Corporate Help Desk will fax or mail the form to the office of your TPA.

Step 7: The Corporate Help Desk will revert to you on the approval status

Emergency Hospitalization: In case of emergency hospitalization, the corporate help desk will take up your case on a fast track basis with your TPA and is likely to receive approval during any working day.

For cashless treatment it is mandatory for the hospital to have an approval from your TPA. In case of delay in receiving the approval or when you cannot wait for receiving the approval owing to medical urgency you can undertake the treatment by paying the necessary cash deposit.

If you receive approval from your TPA after paying the cash deposit, you are entitled for refund of the cash deposit.

CASHLESS FACILITY DENIAL

Cashless hospitalization is linked to the approval of the estimated expenditure on your proposed treatment. In case you do not get your approval you will need to bear the entire expenditure incurred on the treatment. Therefore it is always prudent to get the approval and then get yourself admitted. You could explain the benefits of getting the approval before the date of your admission to your treating doctor as well when he recommends an immediate admission.

Reasons for cashless facility denial

Normally your request for approval might be rejected when:

i.   Information contained in the pre-authorization form is insufficient for the TPA to arrive at a decision and further information is not available for various reasons. However the chances of rejection under this criterion are rare since the Corporate Help Desk at the hospital is experienced in complying with pre-authorization formalities and will advise you suitably

ii.   The ailment for which hospitalization is being sought by you is not covered under your insurance policy for reasons like pre-existing ailment, specific exclusions (accident admission under the influence of alcohol)

iii. You have exhausted your eligible Medical Insurance cover for the year.

iv.   Sometimes cases are being rejected by the TPA for Under evaluation hospitalization whereas per TPA patient was admitted for evaluation purpose only.

v.   Patient/Attendant not able to provide required documents as asked by TPA.

If the actual medical expenses overshoot the pre-approved amount

In case your hospitalization expenses exceed the pre-approved amount, you can approach the Corporate Help Desk to apply for an enhancement of the pre-approved amount. The Corporate Help Desk will apply for an enhancement on your behalf with the TPA and provide the necessary documentation. In case you have not exhausted your medical insurance limit, it is most likely that your TPA will approve the application for the enhancement – either for the requested enhanced amount or up to your insured limit after deducting the value already utilized by you during the year – whichever is less. If the TPA turns down the request for enhancement you will need to pay the amount incurred in excess of your approved amount directly to the hospital before the discharge

Cashless hospitalization cover

For complete details on the medical expenses that are covered, and those that are not covered, you need to go through your health insurance policy. However, in general, the expenses listed below are not reimbursable under cashless hospitalization.

- Registration / Admission Fee

- Telephone Charges

- Visitors / Attendees Charges

- Charges for Diet, which is not part of the administered treatment

- Document Charges

- Toiletries

- Non-medical Expenses

These need to be settled by you directly to the hospital at the time of discharge

STAKE HOLDERS IN HEALTH INSURANCE

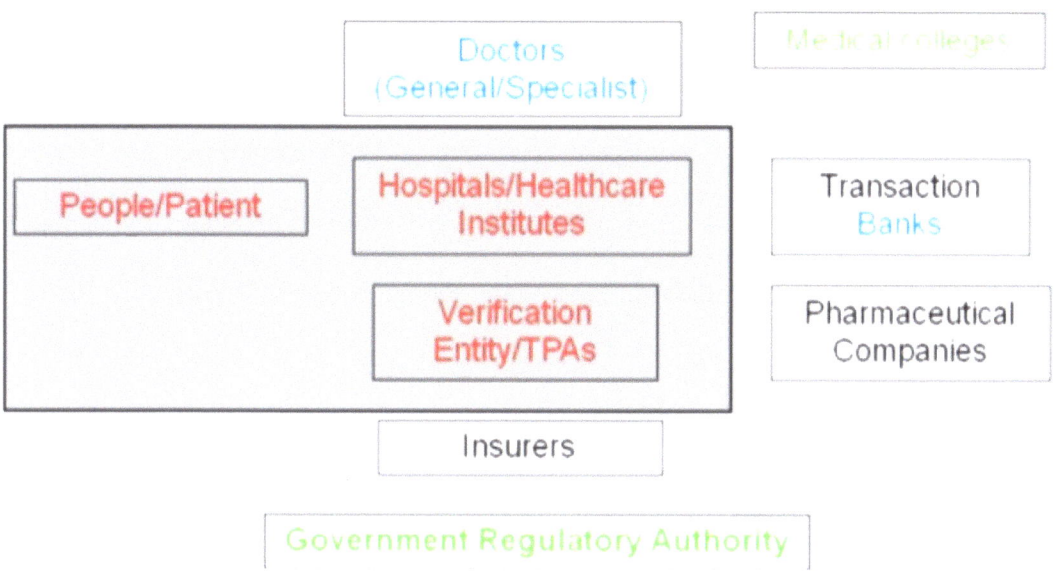

IRDA: Insurance Regulatory & Development Authority, a body constituted under the Ministry of Finance to deal with licensing, regulating and monitoring all activities relating to the insurers, brokers, agents, corporate agents and the TPA's.

TPA: Third party administrators are the new breed of intermediaries in the sector, introduction of whom will benefit both the insured and the insurer. While the insured is benefited by better service, insurers are benefited by reduction in their administrative costs.

Insurers can now outsource their administrative activities, including settlement of claims, to Third party administrators, who offer such services at a cost. It may be noted that TPAs are remunerated by the insurers and so policy holders should welcome such a move since they receive enhanced facilities at no extra cost. Once the policy has been issued, all the records will be passed on to the TPA and all the correspondence of the insured will be with the TPA.

And they will have full-time medical practitioners under their employment who will immediately take a decision on whether the ailment is covered under the policy. TPA license can be granted to any company registered under the companies Act 1956. IRDA, which licenses and regulates these TPAs, has specified stiff entry norms some of which include a minimum capital requirement of 1 Crore, capping the foreign equity at 26% etc.

Partial List of TPAs of India

- TTK HEALTH CARE SERVICES PVT LTD
- MEDI ASSIST INDIA PVT.LTD
- BAJAJ ALLIANZ GENERAL INSURANCE CO LTD.
- E-MEDITEK SOLUTIONS LIMITED
- FAMILY HEALTH PLAN LIMITED
- MEDICARE TPA SERVICES INDIA PVT LTD
- PARAMOUNT HEALTH SERVICES PVT LTD
- UNITED HEALTHCARE INDIA PVT LTD
- GENINS INDIA LTD
- MEDSAVE
- RAKSHA TPA
- M D INDIA
- VIPUL MED CORP
- ALANKIT

- DEDICATED HEALTHCARE SERVICES

- ACCIDENT RELIEF CARE

- GOOD HEALTH PLAN LTD

Insurance Companies

In insurance company, buyers are willing to pay premium to an insurance company that pools people with similar risks and insures them for health expenses. The key distinction is that the premiums are set at a level, which provides a profit to third party and provider institutions. Premiums are based on an assessment of the risk status of the consumer (or of the group of employees) and the level of benefits provided, rather than as a proportion of the consumer's income

Partial List of Insurance Companies of India

Govt Sector

1. Oriental Insurance Company

2. National Insurance Company

3. New India Assurance Company

4. United India Insurance Company

Private Sector

1. ICICI Lombard & ICICI Prudential

2. Max Bupa

3. HDFC ERGO

4. Cholamandalam

5. Bajaj Allianz

6. Reliance Health

7. Royal Sundaram

8. Apollo Munich

Providers (Hospitals)

A hospital is an institution for health care providing treatment by specialized staff and equipment, and often but not always providing for longer- term patient stays. Hospitals are largely staffed by professional physicians, surgeons and nurses.

AIMS & OBJECTIVES OF THIS STUDY

1. To study the current structure & processes of TPA in the hospital.

2. Efficiency of service regarding, turnaround time for getting approvals.

3. To observe the Counseling done to patient by the staff regarding process of Cashless facility and intimation of status of their claim.

4. To seek the views of patients & staff in TPA Deptt.

5. To suggest measures to improve efficiency and patient satisfaction through patient questionnaire and observations made during study.

REVIEW OF LITERATURE

The concept of health insurance was proposed in 1694 by Hugh the Elder Chamberlin from the Peter Chamberlin family. In the late 19th century, "accident insurance" began to be available, which operated much like modern *disability* insurance. This payment model continued until the start of the 20th century in some jurisdictions (like California), where all laws regulating health insurance actually referred to disability insurance. Accident insurance was first offered in the United States by the Franklin Health Assurance Company of Massachusetts. This firm, founded in 1850, offered insurance against injuries arising from railroad and steamboat accidents. Sixty organizations were offering accident insurance in the US by 1866, but the industry consolidated rapidly soon thereafter. While there were earlier experiments, the origins of sickness coverage in the US effectively date from 1890. The first employer-sponsored group disability policy was issued in 1911.

Before the development of medical expense insurance, patients were expected to pay all other health care costs out of their own pockets, under what is known as the fee-for-service business model. During the middle to late 20th century, traditional disability insurance evolved into modern health insurance programs. Today, most comprehensive private health insurance programs cover the cost of routine, preventive, and emergency health care procedures, and also most prescription drugs, but this was not always the case.

Hospital and medical expense policies were introduced during the first half of the 20th century. During the 1920s, individual hospitals began offering services to individuals on a pre-paid basis, eventually leading to the development of Blue Cross organizations. The predecessors of today's Health Maintenance Organizations (HMOs) originated beginning in 1929, through the 1930s and on during World War II.

A Health insurance policy is a contract between an insurance company and an individual. The contract can be renewable annually or monthly. The type and amount of health care costs that will be covered by the health plan are specified in advance, in the member contract or Evidence of Coverage booklet. The individual policy-holder's payment obligations may take several forms

- **Premium:** The amount the policy-holder pays to the health plan each month to purchase health coverage.

- **Deductible:** The amount that the policy-holder must pay out-of-pocket before the health plan pays its share. For example, a policy-holder might have to pay a $500 deductible per year, before any of their health care is covered by the health plan. It may take several doctor's visits or prescription refills before the policy-holder reaches the deductible and the health plan starts to pay for care.

- **Copayment:** The amount that the policy-holder must pay out of pocket before the health plan pays for a particular visit or service. For example, a policy-holder might pay a $45 copayment for a doctor's visit, or to obtain a prescription. A copayment must be paid each time a particular service is obtained.

- **Coinsurance:** Instead of paying a fixed amount up front (a copayment), the policy-holder must pay a percentage of the total cost. For example, the member might have to pay 20% of the cost of a surgery, while the health plan pays the other 80%. Because there is no upper limit on coinsurance, the policy-holder can end up owing very little, or a significant amount, depending on the actual costs of the services they obtain.

- **Exclusions:** Not all services are covered. The policy-holder is generally expected to pay the full cost of non-covered services out of their own pocket.

- **Coverage limits:** Some health plans only pay for health care up to a certain dollar amount. The policy-holder may be expected to pay any charges in excess of the health plan's maximum payment for a specific service. In addition, some plans have annual or lifetime coverage maximums. In these cases, the health plan will stop payment when they reach the benefit maximum and the policy-holder must pay all remaining costs.

- **Out-of-pocket maximums:** Similar to coverage limits, except that in this case, the member's payment obligation ends when they reach the out-of-pocket maximum, and the health plan pays all further covered costs. Out-of-pocket maximums can be limited to a specific benefit category (such as prescription drugs) or can apply to all coverage provided during a specific benefit year.

Prescription drug plans are a form of insurance offered through many employer benefit plans in the US, where the patient pays a copayment and the prescription drug insurance pays the rest.

Some health care providers will agree to bill the insurance company if patients are willing to sign an agreement that they will be responsible for the amount that the insurance company doesn't pay, as the insurance company pays according to "reasonable" or "customary" charges, which may be less than the provider's usual fee. Health insurance companies also often have a network of providers who agree to accept the reasonable and customary fee and waive the remainder. It will generally cost the patient less to use an in-network provider.

Inherent problems with insurance

Insurance systems must typically deal with two inherent challenges: adverse selection, which affects any voluntary system, and ex-post moral hazard, which affects any insurance system in which a third party bears major responsibility for payment, whether that is an employer or the government. Some national systems with compulsory insurance utilize systems such as risk equalization and community rating to overcome these inherent problems.

Adverse selection

Insurance companies use the term "adverse selection" to describe the tendency for only those who will benefit from insurance to buy it. Specifically when talking about health insurance, unhealthy people are more likely to purchase health insurance because they anticipate large medical bills. On the other side, people who consider themselves to be reasonably healthy may decide that medical insurance is an unnecessary expense; if they see the doctor once a year and it costs $250, that's much better than making monthly insurance payments of $40. (example figures).

The fundamental concept of insurance is that it balances costs across a large, random sample of individuals (see risk pool). For instance, an insurance company has a pool of 1000 randomly selected subscribers, each paying $100 per month. One person becomes very ill while the others stay healthy, allowing the insurance company to use the money paid by the healthy people to pay for the treatment costs of the sick person. However, when the pool is self-selecting rather than random, as is the case with individuals seeking to purchase health insurance directly, adverse selection is a greater concern. A disproportionate share of health care spending is attributable to individuals with high health care costs. In the US the 1% of the population with the highest spending accounted for 27% of aggregate health care spending in 1996. The highest-spending 5% of the population accounted for more than half of all spending. These patterns were stable through the 1970s and 1980s, and some data suggest that they may have been typical of the mid-to-early 20th century as well. A few individuals have extremely high medical expenses, in extreme cases totaling a half million dollars or more. Adverse selection could leave an insurance company with primarily sick subscribers and no way to balance out the cost of their medical expenses with a large number of healthy subscribers.

Because of adverse selection, insurance companies employ medical underwriting, using a patient's medical history to screen out those whose pre-existing medical conditions pose too great a risk for the risk pool. Before buying health insurance, a person typically fills out a comprehensive medical history form that asks whether the person smokes, how much the person weighs, whether the person has been treated for any of a long list of diseases and so on. In general, those who present large financial burdens are denied coverage or charged high premiums to compensate. One large US industry survey found that roughly 13 percent of applicants for comprehensive, individually purchased health insurance who went through the medical underwriting in 2004 were denied coverage. Declination rates increased significantly with age, rising from 5 percent for individuals 18 and under to just under a third for individuals aged 60 to 64. Among those who were offered coverage, the study found that 76% received offers at standard premium rates, and 22% were offered higher rates. On the other side, applicants can get discounts if they do not smoke and are healthy.

Moral hazard

Moral hazard occurs when an insurer and a consumer enter into a contract under symmetric information, but one party takes action, not taken into account in the contract, which changes the value of the insurance. A common example of moral hazard is third-party payment—when the parties involved in making a decision are not responsible for bearing costs arising from the decision. An example is where doctors and insured patients agree to extra tests which may or may not be necessary. Doctors benefit by avoiding possible malpractice suits, and patients benefit by gaining increased certainty of their medical condition. The cost of these extra tests is borne by the insurance company, which may have had little say in the decision. Co-payments, deductibles, and less generous insurance for services with more elastic demand attempt to combat moral hazard, as they hold the consumer responsible.

Other factors affecting insurance prices

A recent study by Price Waterhouse Coopers examining the drivers of rising health care costs in the US pointed to increased utilization created by increased consumer demand, new treatments, and more intensive diagnostic testing, as the most significant driver. People in developed countries are living longer. The population of those countries is aging, and a larger group of senior citizens requires more intensive medical care than a young healthier population. Advances in medicine and medical technology can also increase the cost of medical treatment. Lifestyle-related factors can increase utilization and therefore insurance prices, such as: increases in obesity caused by insufficient exercise and unhealthy food choices; excessive alcohol use, smoking, and use of street drugs. Other factors noted by the PWC study included the movement to broader-access plans, higher-priced technologies, and cost-shifting from Medicaid and the uninsured to private payers.

METHODOLOGY

The data was collected from a reputed hospital (Pentamed Hospital, New Delhi)

PENTAMED HOSPITAL

It is a 30 bed multi-specialty Hospital registered with DHS, which has put into practice advanced affordable medical and surgical care. It is one of the first few hospitals to be given ISO 9001:2000 certification in Delhi, is conveniently located in North Delhi in Derawaal Nagar, established & promoted by experienced specialists of the area.

Highlights of facilities being provided by Pentamed hospital

- Experienced & competent dedicated consultants in various specialties & super specialties.

- Well-appointed AC rooms equipped with all modern facilities.

- Fully equipped ICU managed by intensivists.

- Sleep studies & Non invasive cardiac diagnostics facilities.

- State of art operation theatres equipped with C-ARM facility and laminar flow.

- Labour Room for delivery in comfort & with tender care.

- Eyecare and facility for stichless cataract operation by PHACO.

- Lung function testing.

- Round the clock casualty services

- Radio Diagnostics facilities and well equipped Path lab

- Round the clock availability of fully equipped ambulance with advance life support system.

- Healthy & hygienic food, kitchen is being maintained under the supervision of Dietician.

- 100% power back-up, Lift & the hospital is well equipped with fire fighting safety provisions.

Sample size for the study was from the patients who were availing the facility of Cashless in Pentamed Hospital with effect from 8th June 2015 to 10th June 2015.

These patients were given a questionnaire as per preformed to record their response. Structured questionnaire were used. Questionnaire was designed specifically to evaluate the services provided by the TPA Deptt. of the hospital.

OBSERVATIONS

TPA Deptt. /Insurance Desk was located inside the hospital next to billing counter as the patients who come for admissions with cashless card they were guided to this Deptt. Area allotted for Insurance desk was well accessible to all and it was provided with two desks with systems and internet connection, scanner and fax machine connected to the systems. TPA Deptt. of the hospital is headed by Mr.Devender, other than processing of insurance request of the patients TPA Deptt. Also looks after the payments from insurance companies and TPA.

Current Structure and Functioning of the department

Once the doctor advises admission, patient or his attendant carry all the required documents to the TPA Deptt. after confirming the TPA, Hospital staff gets the preauth filled by treating doctor and send all the documents to the concerned TPA, accordingly hospital receives initial approval or query which is informed to the patient/attendant. Query raised can be at patients end requiring policy document or other documents or it can be at hospital end which is replied accordingly. When doctor advice discharge then after preparation of discharge summary then all the documents along with discharge summary and final bill are sent to the TPA for full and final approval, after receiving approval, approval letter along with all documents handed over to patient after all the formalities completed at hospital end. All the documents with a checklist of the concerned patient are then sent to TPA for payment.

Views of the Hospital staff and Insurance Desk Incharge

As per the hospital staff process of TPA Deptt. Looks simple but its actually very complex with so many events occurring at the same time which are to be resolved as early as possible, as patients/ attendants are very much adamant about receiving approval, he also felt that mindset of patient is also different as they consider cashless card as if carrying credit card and they are not pay anything so when approval is not received because of any reason they generally don't accept that easily which inturn results in very less appreciation for their work. These are highlight of work done by the TPA staff.

- After receiving patient cashless card preauth sent to the treating doctor meanwhile patient is informed about the process of cashless facility and non payable items which will be deducted by insurance company.

- On receiving filled preauth other documents along with are sent to the concerned TPA.

- If approval received patient is informed about the status, if query is received then its sent to the treating doctor for reply or to the patient if its to be resolved at his end.

- If case is under process then follow-up is also done by TPA staff from the TPA through system or telephonically.

- When the patient is on discharge, discharge summary along with final bill reaches TPA Deptt. which are sent to TPA again for final approval after cross checking all the documents.

- Once final approval is received admission desk is informed and process of relieving patient starts, approval letter is handed over to patient along with all required documents.

- Now approval letter along with all required documents with a check list of concerned patient are sent to the TPA for payment within 7 days of discharge.

- During patient admission representative of insurance companies visits hospital for verification purposes, TPA Deptt. cooperate with them for conducting their verification.

- Maintain monthly outstanding for the cases processed by TPA Deptt.

- At the end of the day patient sheet handed over to admission desk regarding status of claim and any requirement from the patient.

Following problems are being faced by TPA Deptt.

- Late query, approval receiving from TPA.

- Discharges are received late that is after 3-4hrs of doctor advising discharge.

- Late receiving of required documents from patient/attendant.

- Follow-up of claim status from TPA is very cumbersome.

- Keeping a track of payments received from TPA and regular follow up with them.

DATA ANALYSIS

The data was collected through patient questionnaire and also through records maintained in the hospital. As per the TPA staff in a month average about 110-120 cases are processed on daily basis, this data was received from hospital records regarding processing of cases and payment received for the cases.

Period	Total no. of cases processed	Payment received of the cases from TPA	Payment under process	Payment denied by the TPA
From 1/1/14-31/3/15	1647	1622	25	1

During this study total 9 cases were received for cashless processing between 8th June 2015 to 10th June 2015 , they were given the questionnaire through which following data was obtained to understand the efficiency of the TPA Deptt.

Flowsheet of the patient

S.no.	Reg no.	Name	Age	Sex	Panel/TPA
1	1516-0778	Vaibhav jain	25	M	Raksha
2	1516-0781	Ajay kumar	56	M	Vipul
3	1516-0783	Ankit singhal	28	M	MD India
4	1516-0762	Satish gupta	52	M	MD India
5	1516-0789	Manjeet kaur	70	F	Raksha
6	1516-0748	Ranjit singh	63	M	Medicare
7	1516-0764	Satish goel	59	M	Park
8	1516-0788	Swarn kanta	71	F	Medsave
9	1516-0798	Kapil verma	29	M	Max Bupa

Turnaround time for initial preauth sending

Duration	No. of cases	Percentage
0-1hr	0	0%
1-2hrs	2	22.22%
2-4hrs	4	44.44%
>4hrs	3	33.33%

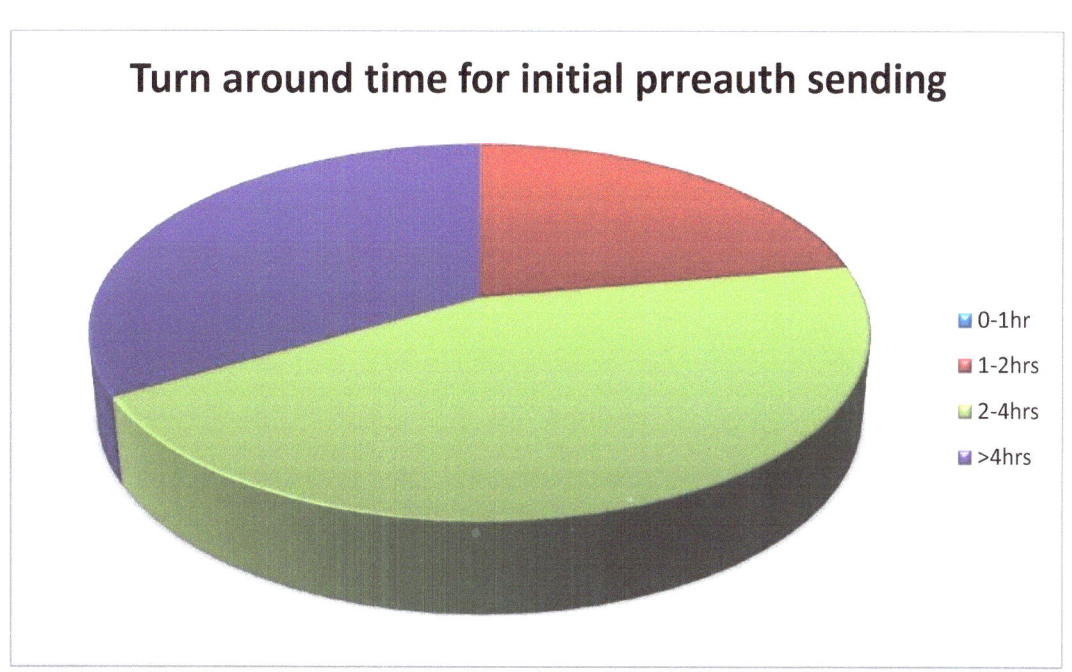

Turnaround time for initial approval or query receiving

Duration	No. of cases	Percentage
0-1hr	0	0%
1-2hrs	2	22.22%
2-4hrs	1	11.11%
>4hrs	6	66.66%

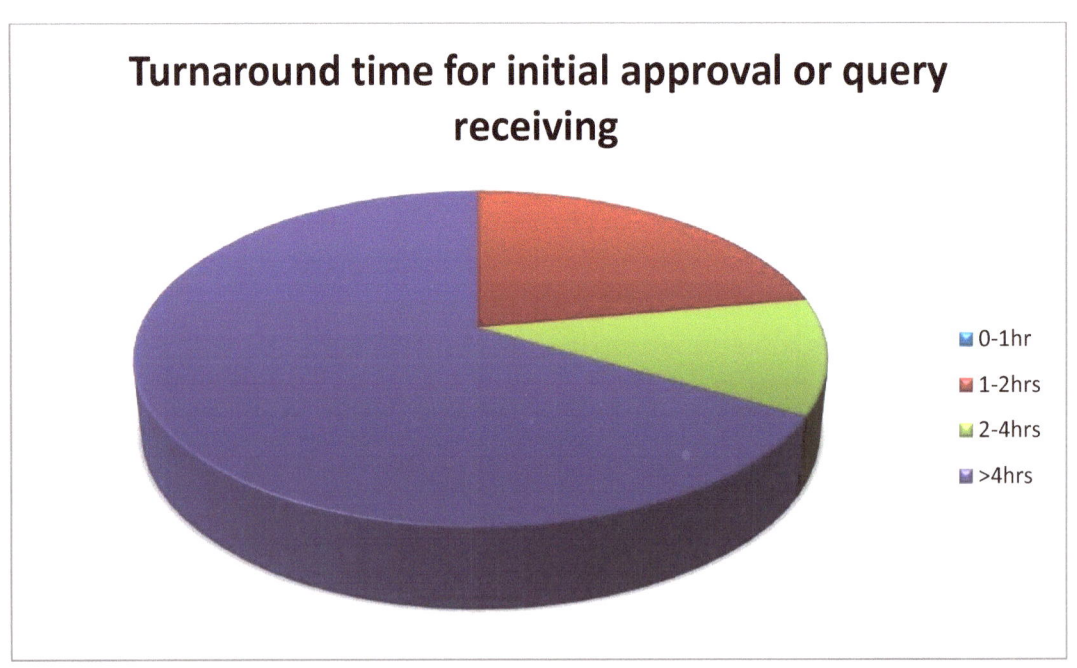

Turnaround time for initial approval or query receiving

- 0-1hr
- 1-2hrs
- 2-4hrs
- >4hrs

Turnaround time for query reply

Duration	No. of cases	Percentage
0-1hr	0	0%
1-2hrs	1	11.11%
2-4hrs	6	66.66%
>4hrs	2	22.22%

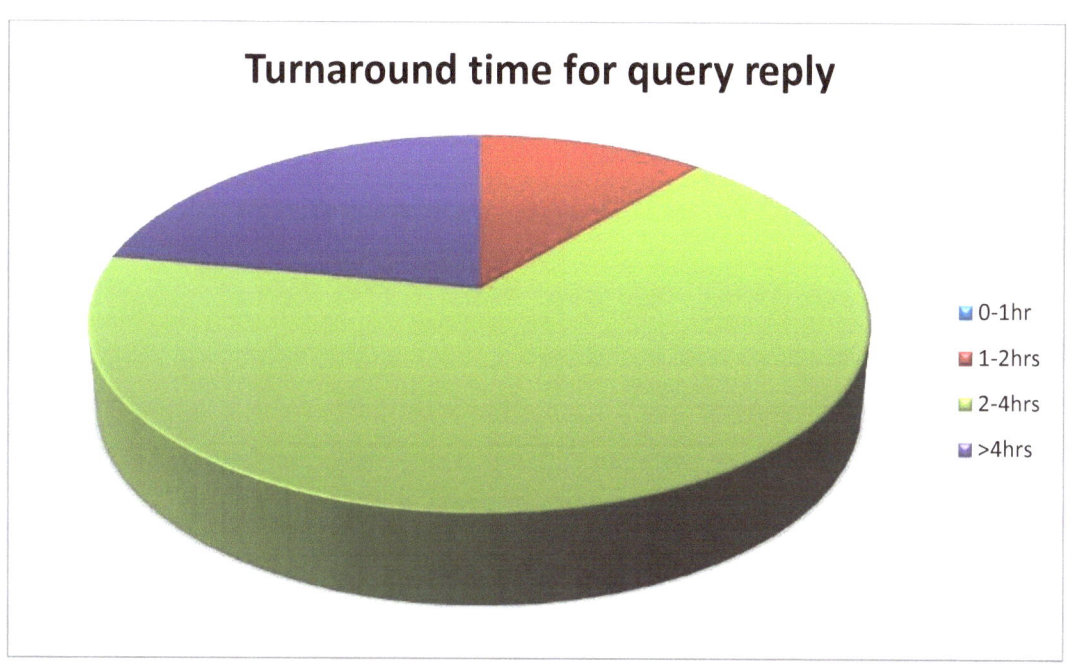

Turnaround time for query reply

Turnaround time for sending discharge summary and final bill after doctor's order

Duration	No. of cases	Percentage
0-1hr	0	0%
1-2hrs	0	0%
2-4hrs	6	66.66%
>4hrs	3	33.33%

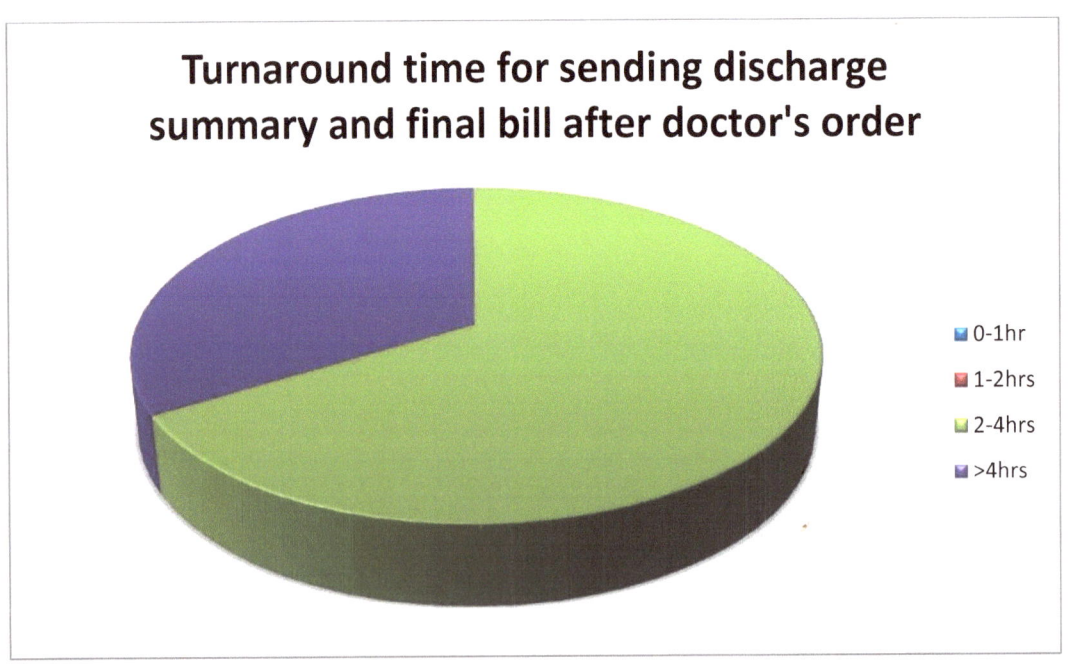

Turnaround time for relieving of patient after receiving final approval

Duration	No. of cases	Percentage
0-15mins	4	44.44%
15-30mins	4	44.44%
30-60mins	1	11.11%
>1hr	0	0%

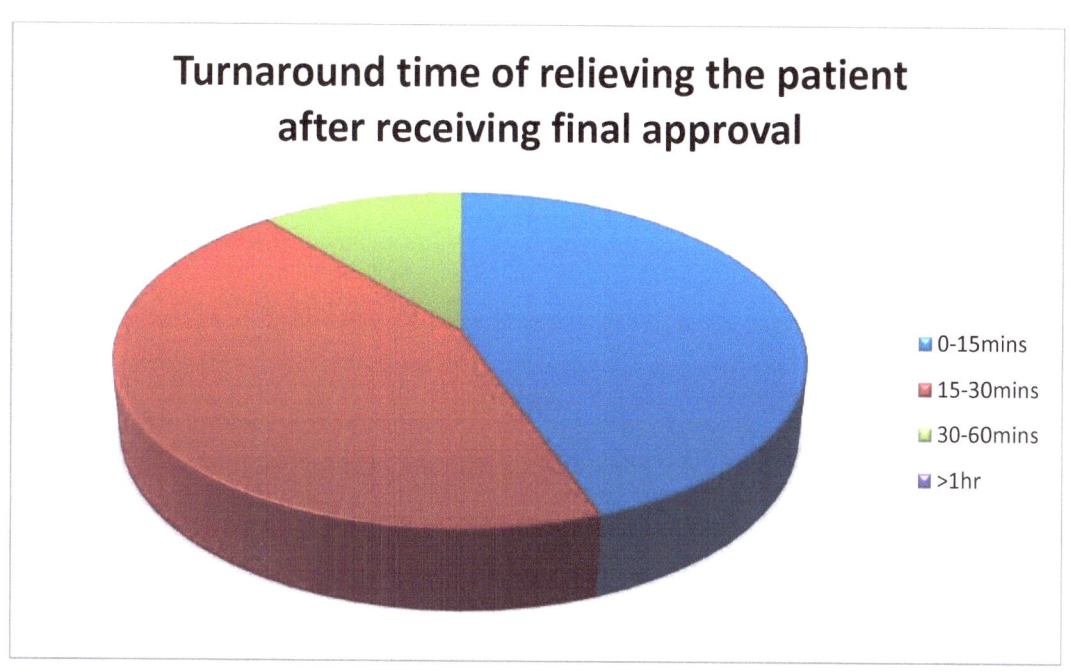

QUESTIONAIRE FOR PATIENTS

Analysis of questionnaires received from the patients or their attendants about the functioning of TPA Deptt.

1. All the patients/ patient attendees felt that the cashless facility was advantageous, as compared to reimbursement facility.

2. 11% patients or attendees felt that reimbursement was better than cashless, 22% felt it was tedious and remaining 67% felt it was not as good as cashless.

3. Turnaround time for initial preauth sending 22% of total cases took 1-2hrs, 44% took 2-4hrs and 33% took more than 4hrs.

4. Turnaround time for initial approval or query receiving 22% of total cases took 1-2hrs, 11% took 2-4hrs and 66% took more than 4hrs.

5. Turnaround time for query reply 11% of total cases took 1-2hrs, 66% took 2-4hrs and 22% took more than 4hrs.

6. Turnaround time for sending discharge summary and final bill after doctor's order 66% of total cases took 2-4hrs and 33% took more than 4hrs.

7. Turnaround time for relieving of patient after receiving final approval 44% of total cases took 0-15mins, 44% took 15-30mins and 11% took 30-60mins.

8. Almost all the patient/attendants were explained about insurance processing and related non medical expenses to be paid by them.

9. Out of 9 patients/attendants 22% felt that their interaction with TPA Deptt. was very good, 44% felt it was good whereas 33% felt it was satisfactory.

DISCUSSION

TPA Deptt. in a hospital is perhaps as important as any other department because key stake holders in the ecosystem namely Patients, Hospitals and also TPAs are related through it, it works like a bridge between them. In the current study it was found that TPA Deptt. of Pentamed hospital found to be very efficient as compared to other hospitals, though TPA Deptt. staff very well handling the pain points in the insurance processing still there were some loop holes observed during the study which should be looked at to improve efficiency and patient satisfaction.

TPA is Deptt. is connected to almost every Deptt. in a hospital, if there is any delay in other Deptt. for completing their job it adversely affects the TAT of TPA Deptt. like delay at admission desk and billing Deptt. for providing final bill which inturn results in delay in sending the final bill and discharge summary for final approval, delay in preparing the discharge summary, delay at doctor's end in replying the query, delay at patient end in providing the required documents as asked y their insurance companies, delay at Lab in providing reports which are required to be sent when a query is raised and so on.

There are few common reasons for denial of cashless and these should be confirmed before sending the patient request.

Normally request for approval might be rejected when:

i.   Information contained in the pre-authorization form is insufficient for the TPA to arrive at a decision and further information is not available for various reasons.

ii. The ailment for which hospitalization is being sought not covered under insurance policy for reasons like pre-existing ailment, specific exclusions (accident admission under the influence of alcohol)

iii. Exhausted eligible Medical Insurance cover for the year.

iv. Sometimes cases are being rejected by the TPA for Under evaluation hospitalization where, as per TPA patient was admitted for evaluation purpose only.

v. Patient/Attendant not able to provide required documents as asked by TPA.

Loopholes in the system

➢ High TAT for sending preauth

➢ High TAT for receiving initial approval

➢ Very high TAT for sending final bill and discharge summary after doctor's advice

➢ Complex procedure followed after doctor's advice for discharge.

Few good initiatives of the TPA Deptt. were also noted during the study

➢ Maintaining of monthly outstanding for the cases processed, its helpful in confirming about the payments pending at TPA end.

➢ Maintaining a follow up sheet of the case from beginning till end, helpful in updating about exact time of all the process done with a case.

➢ Documents after final approval are sent to the TPA with a checklist hence there are less chances of query being raised by the TPA

➢ Adequate knowledge of insurance processing amongst TPA Deptt. staff, less chances of case getting rejected.

➢ Quick disposal of responsibilities by TPA Deptt. staff.

At the end of the study it can be said that TPA Deptt. of Pentamed hospital is very much efficient in handling cashless request of patients only few loopholes are needed to be corrected for more patient satisfaction and also constant improvisation is required in the current structure and service to continue providing better services.

SUGGESTION/RECOMMENDATIONS

- TAT should be reduced for sending preauth and discharge summary, especially when the patient is on discharge, discharge summary and filled preauth should reach the TPA Deptt. within maximum 2hrs after doctor's advice.

- Procedure followed after doctor's advice for discharge should be cut short.

- Constant status update should be intimated to patient/attendant irrespective of approval/query received or not.

- A medical professional can be recruited in the Deptt. especially who has experience in insurance sector and aware of the policy terms and condition as they will provide dual benefit as they can coordinate with treating consultants of hospital and also the Doctors of TPA hence resulting in quicker query reply.

- Online processing of cashless request is started by some TPA should be adopted in the hospital for quick updating of documents and keeping the track record at the same time.

- Reconsideration of request for denied cases as similar to rerequest or enhance.

- While searching for patient the system display at TPA Deptt. should show all processed and unprocessed cases and should be marked with different colours.

- Main emphasis should be on factors which results in rejection of cases they should be minimized before sending patient request.

- The processing should be extended to late hours in the evening and even on holidays and Sundays, more manpower can be recruited for the same depending on the work flow.

- Preauth should be completely filled providing complete information about patient condition as it avoids unnecessary queries and query reply also should be properly answered specific to the question asked.

ANNEXURE: QUESTIONAIRE FOR THE PATIENTS

Name: _____

Age/ Gender: _____

TPA/Insurance company: _____

Corporate: _____

1.	Have you ever availed cashless facility for your treatment in the hospital?
	o YES o NO
2.	What do you feel about availing cashless facility in the hospital?
	o ADVANTAGE o DISADVANTAGE
3.	What do you feel about reimbursement process?
	o Better than cashless o Tedious o Not as good as cashless
4.	What is your previous experience with health insurance?
	o Reimbursement o Cashless by fax method o Cashless by online method
5	Turnaround time for initial Preauth sending?
	o 0-1 hour o 1-2 hours o 2-4 hours o More than 4 hours
6.	Turnaround time for initial preauth approval or query receiving?
	o 0-1 hour o 1-2 hours

	o 2-4 hours	
	o More than 4 hours	
7.	Turnaround time for query reply?	
	o 0-1 hour	
	o 1-2 hours	
	o 2-4 hours	
	o More than 4 hours	
8.	Turnaround time for sending discharge summary and final bill after doctor?	
	o 0-1 hour	
	o 1-2 hours	
	o 2-4 hours	
	o More than 4 hours	
9.	Turnaround time for relieving of patient after receiving final approval?	
	o 0-15 mins	
	o 15-30 mins	
	o 30-60 mins	
	o More than 1 hour	
10	How do you know the status of your cashless claim?	
	o Follow-up with helpdesk	
	o From TPA	
	o From Hospital	
11.	Have you been explained about the Insurance Processing and related Non medical expenses to be paid by you?	
	o Yes	
	o No	
12.	Overall interaction with the Insurance Helpdesk?	
	o Very good	
	o Good	
	o Satisfactory	
	o Bad	

ANNEXURE: CERTIFICATE FROM HOSPITAL

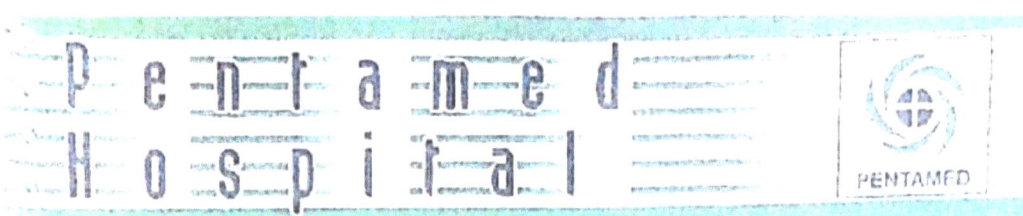

Date: 15.06.2015

CERTIFICATE

This is to certify that work incorporated in this project entitled "A study on structure & functioning of TPA Deptt. (Third Party Administrator) / Insurance Help desk of Pentamed hospital" is an original work and has been undertaken by Dr. Adnan Mastan in our hospital between 8th to 10th June'2015. The procedure & observations embodied in this project has been undertaken by the candidate himself & conducted in our TPA deptt.

For Pentamed Hospital

PENTAMED HOSPITAL
Local Shopping Centre
Derawal Nagar, Ph-IV
Delhi-110009

7, Local Shopping Centre, Derawal Nagar, Gujranwala Town, Phase IV, Delhi-110009
Ph: 47014701 (30Lines)